OWN YOUR
REPUTATION

A Guide to An Online Reputation That Attracts Customers, Clients, Patients, And Followers

by Greg Jordan

B2B Resource Team LLC, Sarasota, Florida

Introduction

"Reputation is an outcome; but it is also a valuable strategic asset."

Andrew Griffin

 "Wow! These folks must be good!" – it's the reaction you want when people see your online star ratings and reviews - Google's always-on-display reputation scorecard.

Created from the opinions of people who we don't even know, these scorecards have a unique power to influence buying decisions. Restaurants, doctors, retailers, hospitals, nonprofits, nursing homes, real estate brokers, departments of motor vehicles, dentists, veterinarians, and any other organization you can think of, participate in this system every day whether they want to or not.

What a business says about its products and services is less important than what current and future customers, patients, or clients say about it. And today they've got plenty to say and an ability to broadcast it on the web with just a few taps on their phone.

5

Business owners know that over time their collection of online reviews, particularly Google reviews, are metrics that future clients, patients and customers pay attention to. Businesses know that a positive online reputation helps to build a brand that people trust and support with their dollars. Some are keenly aware of this and others, not so much.

This book is a guide for local business owners and managers, corporate and nonprofit leaders, and business people who want to take control of their online reputation, and build an enduring brand.

In addition to Google Star Ratings, a brand-building online reputation includes other factors such as:

►**Well Defined Core Values** – Companies that have the integrity to identify and actually live their core values are in such high demand today. When this happens, it shows up in every employee's attitude, and the company's products and services. It's a foundation of the company's brand and reputation. People know with even the briefest of contacts that they're dealing with a company they can trust (or not!).

►**Product and Service Quality** – It all starts here. Give people products and services that they'll want to brag about. High quality products and services are the foundation of a powerhouse online reputation.

►**Search Rankings** - What happens when prospective customers, clients or patients search online using terms related to your business? Where does your business appear on Google's organic Search Engine Results Page (SERP) or ad position? If it's a local business, where does it appear in Google's local listings? A business whose website, articles and content are highly ranked differentiates itself as an authority in its industry.

►**Clear, Consistent Brand Message** – If Google star ratings are a gauge of how customers experience the business, consistent brand messaging helps to communicate what people should know and feel about it. Do people understand and believe what your core values, products and services can do for them? Do they know what to expect? A consistent, clear brand message is a shorthand for who the business is, its values and its offerings.

►**Purposeful Online Content** – Your website is a 24-hour sales force. Is your website content engaging enough that it helps people understand how the business might solve their problem, meet their needs or bring them happiness? What's said about the business on social media and web pages should help convert prospects to customers, and be in sync with its online reputation.

In the coming chapters, we'll connect these factors into the work of building an online star rating because together they make up the total reputation picture.

A good online reputation, as measured by the average star rating, is to a large degree an outcome of the way the business performs. But reputations can also be improved by working directly on them.

For example, how many 5-star Google reviews are right now in the heads of customers, patients and clients, but haven't been posted - simply because they haven't been asked, or reminded?

Many people don't take the time, don't know how, or haven't been encouraged to write a simple review - even though happy customers are quite willing to do that.

At the other end of the playing field are angry or frustrated customers (hopefully very few). They seem to always have plenty of reason, plenty of time, and need little encouragement to write scalding, emotional reviews aimed at an offending business. Any business can become a victim of the sharp online sword of a frustrated customer even if they don't deserve it.

How much difference can additional Google 5-star reviews make for a business? We'll show later that it can be significant. And we'll explore ways to inspire people to want to write reviews, and how to make it easy for them to do so.

We'll talk about ways to handle negative reviews to your advantage, and why all of that is important.

We'll combine the elements of brand journalism and social media with the work of getting more, positive reviews in a way that creates an amazing brand – one that attracts more customers, clients, patients and followers.

We want this book to help you keep in mind our reputation mantra:

Love your customers,

Respect your competitors,

Leverage your reputation with both.

There are lots of platforms that allow reviews and testimonials to be posted for your business. Facebook, Bing, Yahoo, Yelp and Yellow Pages are just a few examples. And there are also hundreds of special, niche directories and networks that display reviews like the Better Business Bureau, Zillow for real estate, or Health Grades for the medical profession.

All directories play a part in creating your online reputation, but we'll focus on Google reviews because that's where the majority of people find information about people and business. For example, when is the last time you went to an authority site like the local Chamber of Commerce, or even a Facebook page, to check a company's reputation? Answer: most people don't – they go to Google. Nevertheless, the principles in this book apply to most any directory.

We're also making an assumption that the quality of your products and services is in sound shape. The techniques in this, or any other book, will produce no results if the business delivers poor products and services.

If your business is in that situation, you'll need to fix it first.

The case study we've included at the end is meant to be an example of one of the most challenging business niches to get reviews. You'll see why. **The lessons from this case study tell you that it's possible and right for every business to grow their online reputation.**

It's my intent to spark interest and new ways of thinking about your online reputation as an integral part of brand building. Taking action will result in a higher degree of customer loyalty and more revenue.

The solutions we offer follow a simple model:

- ►Build it
- ►Show it
- ►Manage it

Putting in place the details of this model can profoundly affect your brand. It won't be a cure-all, or the final word. However, following just some of its guidance can tip the scales in your favor.

How to Use This Book

The book is designed to serve as a tool to meet your needs. I recommend you read all of the chapters in order, but you can read it in a different order. Take a look through the table of contents and at your option, navigate to the sections that are of most interest.

The core message is about taking control of your own online reputation – owning your reputation - so that it becomes a long-lasting and ever-increasing business generator – even with the occasional negative review.

Building your reputation takes time and work initially, but if done right, the effort required will lessen, and in a shorter time than you might imagine, it could make you proud of how much better your online reputation is than your competitors.

The good news is that it isn't necessary to do everything, or do it all at once. The key is to define your reputation goals, develop a plan, and execute it consistently using your available resources. Only do those things that make the most sense for your business.

The alternative is to accept whatever anyone else wants to do with your reputation.

Which will you choose?

To your success,

Greg Jordan

Why An Online Reputation Is So Important

"It takes 20 years to build a reputation and five minutes to ruin it. If you think about that, you'll do things differently.

-Warren Buffett

Twenty years ago, a business's reputation relied mainly on what people said about it via word of mouth. Eventually, word would get back to the manager or owner and be dealt with accordingly. That was pretty much how business owners managed their reputation.

Today, the internet has made it possible for word of mouth to spread instantly and everywhere online. It's a good bet that at this very moment people are talking about your company on social media, posting reviews, creating hashtags and in some cases, even websites – all to share their opinion about your company, product or service.

The smartphone was the ideal partner for building the online review society we have today. Through these devices, platforms like Amazon, Google, Facebook and others made it easy for people to publish and read reviews anywhere and anytime.

These companies went one step farther and made reviews an important part of their business model.

All of this created our current culture where people are empowered to leave a review for any experience they have. Businesses are no longer solely in charge of their reputation.

The really simple reason online reputations, as measured in overall review scores, is so important is shown in the image below:

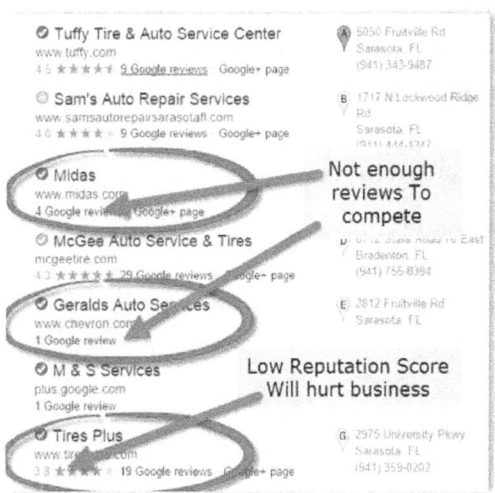

78% of Internet users conduct product research online

80% had a change in purchase decision after seeing a negative review online.

looking for the best reputations as reflected in online reviews.

The major trusted source for reviews is Google. Sure, there are other review platforms like Facebook, Yelp, Yahoo and numerous other directory sites, but there's no getting around the importance of having excellent Google reviews.

To manage an online reputation, you'll need to have a process to:

- ▶Monitor what people say about the business

- ▶Continuously collect reviews

- ▶Respond to reviews

- ▶Market the really good ones

You'll not only need to concern yourself with what people are saying about your business locally, but possibly around the world.

When products or companies have bad reviews, customers will likely steer clear of them. After all, who wants to subject themselves to a possible negative experience?

Likewise, customers will also be wary of companies that don't have an online reputation at all – meaning those that have no, or few reviews and star ratings. In this case, customers, patients and clients don't know what to expect and they'll naturally gravitate to a business with a better reputation.

And here's the worst part. After reading bad reviews about a restaurant, chiropractor, gym, auto repair place, bank or other business, people don't call the business and say: *"Hey, I read your bad reviews online and decided to spend my money with your competitor."*

In other words, you may not be aware that you're losing customers and revenue from a bad online reputation.

Thankfully, it's getting easier to put systems in place to grow, market and manage your online reputation. We'll discuss more about that later.

But first let's review two fundamentals that are connected to online reputation success: business excellence, and how online review scores relate to sales.

Business Excellence: Building Quality into Products and Services

After reading bad reviews about a restaurant, chiropractor, gym, auto repair place, bank or other business, people don't call the business and say: *"Hey, I read your bad reviews online and decided to spend my money with your competitor."*

It all starts with providing your clients, customers or patients with products and services that they love. It seems obvious but it's worth saying that no matter how hard you try, there won't be positive reviews if the products and services aren't good. Getting more reviews for a business that doesn't perform well only highlights its shortcomings.

The first priority then, is to make sure that the majority of customers have an excellent experience. Find the root of any operational problems and systematically fix them, starting with the most critical ones.

Each business will have its unique quality challenges. Employee training, supplier reliability, customer service, employee compensation, manufacturing quality, or leadership and accountability issues are just a few examples of potential issues.

Product and service quality fixes are beyond the scope of this book. But here's a simple framework to begin to identify barriers to improving your reputation:

You'll need to ask and answer questions like:

►What customer value do you offer, and what kind of feedback do you get from them?

►Do you have employees and managers that are knowledgeable and trained in delivering your products and services?

►Is the product or service quality high enough to delight your customers, clients or patients?

►Do your suppliers deliver reliably and with good quality?

►Are staff rewarded enough, so that they'll want to stay and help grow the business?

►Are there clear roles and accountabilities so there's no confusion in operations or projects?

►Are there core values, a vision, goals and an operating plan that everyone understands and aligns to?

Failure to address gaps in these areas, could shorten the life or growth of the business.

I use online shoe sales company, Zappos as one of my favorite benchmarks of excellence. I've always been impressed by their light, friendly personal touch with customers. Even their logo tells you that they're all about providing the best in products and services.

Zappos' customer service response numbers back up their words. Their online customer service response time is less than 20 minutes, with a response rate of

100% - in other words, they respond to their customer's needs very quickly.

Zappos converts their customers into enthusiastic fans and that means plenty of repeat business and a brand-building online reputation. You don't have to be in ecommerce to want to model some of that kind of excellence. It is reputation building at its finest.

At the same time, we realize that no business will be able to deliver 100% satisfaction. There will always be customers, clients, or patients that you won't be able to satisfy, no matter what you do.

Business excellence is the first place to start in building a great online reputation. Correct any problems that would cause customers to leave negative reviews.

Reviews Affect Sales and Outcomes

It's a simple equation: positive online reputations create trust and encourage people to try and purchase. Negative online reputations create skepticism and resistance to engage.

So, what is a positive reputation? In some ways, it depends on the review culture of the specific industry.

One of my clients is in an industry that has for years been the subject of sensational negative press and a reputation for spotty service. The average score of their competitors in that area was well below 4 stars.

In that case, just a 4.0 rating could create a significant reputation advantage. But I don't recommend doing just enough to edge competitors – although that's not a completely unsound strategy.

The next image shows another example of a business (Sam's Auto Repair Services) that may be losing customers to a competitor because they just don't have as much "reputation juice".

Sam's Auto Repair Service
www.samsautorepairsarasotafl.com/ ▾   (941) 315-2148
Service To All Auto Makes & Models. ASE Certified. Work Guaranteed.
♀ 2525 17th Street, Sarasota, FL

    Contact Us   Air Condition Services
    Brake Services   Specials

Auto repair - ServiceKing.com
www.serviceking.com/AutoRepair ▾   (866) 730-5464
We are commited to making repairs as painless as possible. Call Now!
Lifetime Warranties · Wreck Erasers · Insurance Experts Await
Schedule an Appointment · Service King News · Employment Opportunities
♀ 4040 North Washington Blvd, Sarasota, FL

Auto Repair - Ashton Auto Center in Sarasota
www.ashtonautocenter.com/ ▾
Voted Best Auto Repair Shop 4 Yrs
♀ 4502 McAshton Street, Sarasota, FL · (941) 921-4570

Beiler's Auto Repair
www.autorepairservicesarasota.com
5.0 ★ ★ ★ ★ ★ 25 Google reviews · Google+ page

Not enough reviews, lower rating

Sam's Auto Repair Services
www.samsautorepairsarasotafl.com
4.3 ★ ★ ★ ★ ✫ 6 Google reviews · Google+ page

A 5820 Palmer Blvd
(941) 479-3650

B 1717 N Lockwood Ridge Rd
Sarasota, FL
(941) 444-1247

21

As an aside, it also shows how Sam's can partly offset this by paying for Google ads that place them at the very top of the page – but they still have very few reviews relative to their competitor.

In my view, every business should be aiming for a rating average of 4.7 or above with a minimum of 50 reviews. A 4.7 score can build confidence in the business. Unless its competitors are at 4.9.

Why not go for a rating of 5.0? As a lofty vision, that's fine, but it may not be practical to achieve. Mistakes and bad days are inevitable. When that happens, the most important thing people want to see is how the business responds to negative reviews.

In addition, a 5.0 reputation may also be viewed with suspicion. People wonder if a 5.0 business is manipulating its scores somehow.

Generally anything above a 4.7 score with the number of reviews around at least 30 demonstrates a commitment to keeping a tight, customer-centric ship. But the number of reviews and average star rating will be viewed in the context of industry averages, and those of the nearest competitors.

A local business with 30 reviews in an industry where the average number of reviews is 100 will be viewed as non-competitive. Pay attention to the industry, and compare each business to industry and competitor averages.

In deciding what your reputation goals are, it's helpful to think about these questions: What if you could have two, three, or even four times more positive reviews than your competition? How much difference would that make in attracting new business and keeping existing customers?

The Sales Effect

It may not take very much to move the sales needle. Take a look at this statistic from the University of California, Berkeley for an increase of .5 stars.

Positive Yelp Ratings Can Boost A Restaurant's Nightly Reservations by 19%

Economists at the University of California. Berkeley published the results of a study, examining the effects of Yelp's online ratings in this month's *Economic Journal. The study shows a slight half-star improvement in ratings can increase a restaurant's business during peak dining hours by 19%.*

Berkeley professors Michael Anderson and Jeremy Magruder found that "Yelp ratings affect both customer flows and the probability of booking a reservation." The researchers compared the digital word-of-mouth reviews on Yelp of 328 San Francisco eateries with the frequency of nightly reservations at each establishment.

This demonstrates the power of rating stars, whether it's Yelp, Google, or other platforms.

Average star rating and number of reviews should take its place as a critical part of the business marketing strategic plan. It's at the core of the business brand.

Before buying, consumers and business buyers will go online to find reviews and read what people say about products, services, or businesses. Even when they're referred by a trusted source, there's a good chance they'll search the business anyway, if for no other reason than finding the location or phone number.

Every one of these searches can reveal the star rating and number of reviews, and become part of a purchase decision.

Managers and employees need to understand that building positive reviews and reputations is a long-term game. With few exceptions, every review - positive or negative - is on the web forever.

Build A Reputation That People Trust

"If people like you they will listen to you, but if they trust you, they will do business with you".

- Zig Ziglar

Let's start this section with an understanding of common challenges in building an online reputation. Spoiler alert: they're all solvable.

11 Common Online Reputation Challenges

There can be hundreds of things ruining an online reputation. These are the most important ones we see.

1) Poor product and services. Every business gets a bad review from time to time. But as a general rule, if a business's review average is consistently below 4, there are troubles ahead unless they can get it to 4.7 or better. This metric can be industry dependent. Some industries have typically low or high averages. Nonetheless achieving a rating above 4.7 could be a real differentiator.

2) Being Unaware. A business that pays no attention to its reputation, or doesn't know how to monitor it, is in for a rough journey. Some don't care because they're lucky enough to be one of the few suppliers of a particular product or service. Others have no idea that they need to find out. They have no understanding of how much business they may be losing.

Why don't they know? Because prospective customers don't call up to let them know they are not going to do business with them. There's no excuse for not knowing what your online reputation is. It's vitally important that you do.

3) No Review Collecting, Monitoring and Marketing System. Most businesses still don't have a system in place to build and manage their reputation. Their accountants watch their finances, their Human Resources watch their recruiting, their managers watch their operations, but sadly many businesses don't bother to watch and manage their important review assets.

4) Employees not fully invested in getting reviews. In many companies, employees are not trained, and/or are not expected to collect or respond to reviews from customers, clients or patients. If employees are not taught that reviews are important, opportunities to build the brand's reputation escape, and that means lost revenue. Ironically, the employees suffer from this kind of issue when sales losses mount and jobs are cut.

5) The company does not embrace the gift of negative reviews. Negative reviews bring with them the silver cloud of opportunity. Rather than seeing a negative review as a problem or something to be feared, enlightened business owners see it as an opportunity to become stronger and better. As long as negative reviews are a small percentage of total reviews, they provide important feedback to fix the cause of trouble.

6) Hate sites. Hate sites pop up only in the most extreme cases, and it's getting harder for haters to do this because of additional scrutiny on these practices.

It does happen though. If a company has angered someone, or a group of people, to the point that they want to go very public with it, they may go to the trouble of creating a website with the sole purpose of damaging the company's online reputation.

Hate sites can be filled with false negative reviews about your brand, service, or product;

negative testimonials, and more damaging material. They can do extreme harm to your brand. Luckily, they can be taken down. You just have to find them and follow a removal process.

7) Competitive attacks. It used to be unheard of for companies to mention their competitors by name but today it's becoming more and more common, especially in the online world. Many businesses aren't afraid to cross ethical boundaries to say negative things about their own competitors, which might be your business. An example is Bud Light's latest commercials portraying Coors Light and Miller Light negatively for using corn syrup in their brewing processes. They're all in court now. These types of attacks can often be forced to be taken down.

8) Bad press. Bad press can happen more easily than many business owners think and if it does, it can ruin a company. Imagine for instance, the construction companies who installed cheaper Chinese drywall several years ago. That drywall turned out to be a dangerous health problem and as a result, many contractors were blamed and sued.

Bad press can follow a company online for a long time after the initial situation occurs. Potential customers might be able to see it years down the road when they're searching for your company or product.

9) False information. In a search for your company's mentions, you'll most likely come across some things that simply aren't true. This happens for two reasons.

The first is that sometimes, one person will say something about a company to someone else, and as the story is told, it loses a little accuracy. This happens often in social media, and the end result can be detrimental to the brand.

The other type of false information you might come across has been posted maliciously by someone who thinks they've been wronged by the company, such as a disgruntled former employee. These individuals might post lies or exaggerations just to harm your reputation. There's usually a process to get it removed.

10) Hackers. Individuals that pretend to be you online are hackers. Often, they set up social media profiles or websites under your or your company's name.

This presents a number of problems, the first being that when it's time for you to create social media profiles you won't be able to, because your business name has been hijacked. And you might not be able to start a website for your business or brand either, because someone has already purchased the domain name for it.

Once hackers have that kind of control over your brand's name, they can use it to say things that are completely untrue, or that misrepresent the company.

11) Trademark infringement. This happens quite often online, especially on social media. Sometimes those infringing on the trademark are well aware of it, while other times they aren't. Either way, if you find yourself in this situation, a trademark lawyer can help you decide what the right next steps are.

There are two types of responses to any negative or malicious reviews:

▸ Victims, who are at the mercy of whatever reviews and online shenanigans people decide to do to them.

▸ Proactive adaptors, who take charge of their online reputation, figuring out how to tip the scales of online reviews in their favor.

The key is for each business to take control of its reputation and treat it as the asset it is.

Which type is your business?

The rest of this book will be focused on taking control through best practices in reputation management, starting with how to get reviews. And then we'll move on to other important supporting elements that build a brand's reputation.

Best Practices

An online reputation that builds a trusted brand begins with earning lots of 5-Star reviews.

Some of my clients have been able to multiply their number of online reviews by a factor of 10 by following the practices in this chapter. It's helped them stand out from their competitors.

Based on three years of working with multiple clients' reputations, we've developed a list of best review practices. Put all or some of these in place and you're bound to improve your online reputation.

Eight Online Review Best Practices

1) The organization's commitment to the importance of reviews must be clear, and backed by goals and actions. There needs to be a clear understanding that getting reviews is a long-term brand-building strategy. People at the highest levels of the organization need to be involved in getting reviews. Ownership or leadership needs to set expectations that collecting reviews is an important part of the job.

Home Health Care Provider Grannie Nannies of Sarasota (48 reviews, 4.9 stars) is a great example of ownership involvement. Their team proactively looks for family and patients who have had positive experiences, and who also have a Gmail account. The owner then personally follows up with the patient and asks them for their review.

Every employee can see by his example that great service and 5-Star reviews are important to the business. By the way, senior care is one of the most difficult niches for online review success for a number of reasons, and he's having quite a bit of success.

2) Ask everyone that uses, or is familiar with your products and services if they would be willing to give a review. The best at this never let an opportunity to ask for a review pass by without asking, and they do it without annoying their customers. They let them know that they really care about their experience. They stress that feedback helps create better products and services for others and helps to spread the word about how well the business does in meeting customer needs.

I still see a reluctance for some people to ask for reviews. This seems to be particularly true for professionals who dismiss the importance of this simple act. It's almost as though it's below them to make such a request. They'll need to get over that quickly, or fall behind competitors that do get it. Gathering feedback should be seen as an important opportunity to build the brand.

3) Continuously monitor the web. It's important to always be aware of what's being said on the web about your business. Technology makes this easier to do than you might think. Since anyone can write a review at any time, a good mantra is Early Detection and Rapid Response. Companies on top of their reputation know immediately when there's a new review, and respond quickly.

4) Respond to reviews in a way that builds customer confidence. Companies with close to a 5-star reputation understand that a simple "thank you" response to a customer's review is good but misses a big opportunity. They respond in a way that connects with the individual's comment and at the same time, shares the fact that they really care. Their responses to customers are human, engaging, sometimes funny, and done in a way that builds real relationships with people.

The incredible power of responding to reviews in a professional, helpful manner is that the review reader gets a glimpse of what it would be like to do business with you. It's one of the most effective and free forms of advertising there is.

5) Share the news with customers and employees. Share those 5-star reviews proudly on social media, the website and in print. Making a customer happy is what having a value-added business is all about. The more good news is shared, the more confidence it gives to people looking for your services and products. It's also a great opportunity to acknowledge and reward the contribution of employees.

6) Companies that have review request systems have an advantage because these systems automate, and make more efficient, the process of getting reviews and monitoring the web. These systems send email or SMS review requests, and gently follow up with customers if they forget. Having a system shows customers that you care and increases the chances of getting reviews.

7) Use the simple Connect Conversation with prospective reviewers to get a better response

to feedback requests. What is the Connect Conversation? It's one held at a point immediately after the customer, patient or client's experience. It goes something like this:

Business: "How did it go today?"

Customer: "Great!"

Business: "Later today or tonight or whenever you get a chance, would you mind taking a few minutes to write a review for us on Google?"

Business: (Optional) "The reason I ask is because when you give us a review online, it helps others learn about our business through your experience with us."

Customer: "Sure I'd be happy to"

Business: (if they have a review request system) "Before you go, may I send you an email with a link that makes it easy for you to write your review?" or, "May I enter your smart phone in our system so it sends you instructions?"

Business: (if no review request system) "Here's a card for you with instructions on how to leave a review on Google."

Customer: "OK, thanks."

Business: "Thank you so much, and I want you to know that we're all really looking forward to reading your comments. Bye!"

Here are the reasons that the Connect Conversation makes it more likely that patients, clients and customers will give you a review:

► You caught them having a good experience with your products and services while it's fresh in their minds. Happy customers will go the extra mile to help your business, when asked.

► You have gotten their permission to participate in the review process.

► They have personally and directly committed to give you a review.

► You've set the expectation that the business is really interested in their individual opinion and waiting to see their review. How's that for encouragement to keep their word?

It's not always possible to have face-to-face contact with every customer for this conversation. But, do it if you can. The direct personal interaction will get you more reviews than the colder email or text message request.

This is a simple conversation, loaded with subtle psychological triggers, that gets more actual responses. Modify it so it fits your business, and sounds natural to your customers.

Of course, if the patient indicates that they're not satisfied, you have a decision to make. It may be best to refer them to someone who can handle their complaint rather than ask them for a review.

8) Don't game the system. Understand that Google's purpose is to give users the best online experience possible. For years, they have been tightening their rules to penalize businesses who use "black hat" tactics to cheat the system – and that includes fake reviews.

Avoid stuffing your Google My Business or Maps pages with employee reviews (seen by Google as a conflict of interest), fake reviews, buying reviews or any other tricks to get reviews.

Eventually Google catches up with these fabrications, and they'll take drastic measures if the offenses are serious enough. This may include de-indexing your site, deleting reviews or blocking your account. It's not worth the risk. Instead, get reviews the honest way and your business will naturally benefit.

Reviews Are a Numbers Game

As discussed earlier, when a business has few reviews, it presents only a slightly better impression than negative reviews. Simple math shows why the number of reviews becomes a huge factor in these cases.

A business with one 1-star review and one 5-star review has a total of two reviews with an average rating of 3.0 – poor by any standard.

But if you add ten 5-star reviews to that same business, the average score shown in searches will be 4.3 - starting to get respectable. If you add another five 5-star reviews your average score is 4.6 – much better!

The solution for a business with a small number of reviews, or a low average is obvious – create more positive reviews!

Positive Power From Negative Reviews
It sounds odd, but on the way to becoming a perfect business, you need some negative reviews. We'll discuss this in more detail later, but it's important to mention it here.

Honest, negative reviews provide information that helps make the enterprise better. This speaks to the need to use reviews for one of its fundamental purposes: getting feedback to correct problems in the business.

An occasional negative review, even though it may be tough to hear, offers as much value as getting another 5-star review, assuming the business makes a committed effort to act on constructive feedback.

It's pretty much impossible to remove negative online reviews unless they are the kind left by disgruntled former employees or other false, malicious reviews. If you have these issues, there are online organizations that may be able to help remove these types of reviews. But your best bet is to contact Google first.

Most people care more about the way a business responds to a 1-star review than they do about the negative review itself. Responding to the nastiest review professionally, and with an honest commitment to right wrongs, elevates the business in the eyes of other review readers.

What's the secret to turning negative reviews into positive revenue? Respond to the reviewer professionally and publicly online to attempt to make it right. And then gather a mountain of positive reviews from real, satisfied customers, clients or patients.

Don't just respond to negative reviews, either. Aside from the feel-good nature of responding to positive reviews, doing so creates an amazing strategic tool for the business that can't be found anywhere else: broadcasting how much you value your customers, and including related brand messages. It's free "fuel" for the brand.

Take for example a positive review that someone leaves online like "this was the best boarding experience I've ever had." Rather than a simple "thank you", if the pet boarding company responds with "Our staff just loves all of our pet guests, and we look forward to having you and Fluffy back again.", people can feel the warmth, care, and professionalism in the response. Over time, responses like this accumulate into a strong positive brand image in the minds of pet owners.

Respond To Reviews In These Ways To Boost Your Reputation

Once you're getting more reviews, you're ready for one of the best secrets to building your brand's reputation online. It's also one of the simplest acts you can do: Take 15 minutes each day to find and reply to online reviews about the business.

Most businesses don't do this – it doesn't seem to make the high priority list. But this one activity can quickly make the business stand out from competitors in the minds of review readers. Done regularly it becomes a powerful marketing strategy.

The majority of reviews online aren't responded to – including very damaging reviews. The gold standard is to respond to every negative review and as many positive reviews as possible.

Doing this gives people a feeling of confidence even if they've never done business with you. And that's a head start in the race for new clients, customers and patients.

Furthermore, Google likes the engagement. They view review replies as fresh new content and it's likely to have a positive effect on search engine rankings. Recently, Google also enabled the use of hashtags in review responses. In your responses, use your business, product, and service names in hashtags which can help people find your business. So be sure to include relevant hashtags in reviews.

At the time of this writing, Google is also rolling out the ability to post your 5-Star Reviews on Google My Business (GMB). More on GMB later.

Below are some response phrases that work well when responding to reviews. Modify them with your own style and use them as brand-building responses to online (or any) feedback. Notice as you read through them:

- ►The personable nature of the responses

- ►The ownership of mistakes and errors

- ►The commitment to creating a better experience

- ►Relationship building

- ►The invitation to return as customers or to refer others.

Review Response Scripts

1) Thank you, (first name) for this great review! We're glad to hear that you enjoyed our community. Please stop in and say hello when you return. We love the opportunity to meet our family of customers.

2) (First name), thank you so much for taking the time to write a review; we appreciate your feedback and your confidence in us. We are honored to provide (services) to you and we're so proud of our team members!

3) Thank you for the kind words about (employee). We are so pleased to have her as a part of the team and glad she was able to bring you an exceptional experience.

4) Hi (first name), we really appreciate this great review. We work hard to make sure that our customers have a 5-star experience. And, it looks like we were able to do that with you…YAY!! If we can be of any further help, please let us know, and if you would be so kind to share your experience with others, it would be just great!

5) Please accept our sincerest apologies for (problem). We would love the chance to make this right and would like to invite you back to (business) for x % off your next visit.

6) When a customer takes the time to leave a review online, we listen! We want to apologize for (problem) and let you know that we have taken the necessary steps to ensure that this doesn't happen again. Please know that your experience was an isolated occurrence and that the management and staff would love another chance to impress you.

7) It is our goal to treat every person that walks through our doors as a VIP customer. When our team falls short of that standard, and a customer walks away dissatisfied, then we have a real problem. We want to apologize for your less-than-outstanding experience and would like to invite you back to show you just how amazing our team can be.

8) We hear you loud and clear! Your feedback is more than understandable. We appreciate that you took the time to let us know, and we will be implementing your suggestions in the near future. Visit us again to see what a difference your review made.

9) We greatly value the opinions of our customers. At (business) we work hard every day to ensure that our customers' needs are being met. Thank you very much for your review.

10) Everyone has an off day - even amazing businesses. I'd like to apologize for this unfortunate (incident/confusion/inconvenience). Please give us a second chance and see the stuff we are really made of. Visit us again and receive a (%) off your next visit.

11) We apologize for the unfortunate experience and regret that it happened at all. Our #1 goal is customer satisfaction. While we can apologize for this unfortunate situation, sometimes that's just not enough to say we are sorry. We invite you to contact our store manager at (555) 555-5555 and let us know how we can make it up to you.

12) It's understandable that you would be upset after (experience). We definitely do not want to lose you, or anyone, as a customer as a result of this bad experience. Please contact our store manager at (555) 555-5555 and let us know how we can better serve you.

13) Your opinion is very valuable to us at (business). We take each and every customer suggestion into consideration. Thank you very much for your review.

14) A dissatisfied customer is rare and we take your feedback very seriously. Please accept our deepest apology for your unfortunate experience.

Customers will appreciate these kinds of responses and you'll look like the professional that they want to do business with.

Shift Your Reputation Into High Gear with An Online Review Management System (ORMS)

An ORMS is designed to automate the tasks of collecting, monitoring, and marketing reviews. It shortens the timeline to achieving a competitive edge online reputation.

The next image shows how a typical ORMS works:

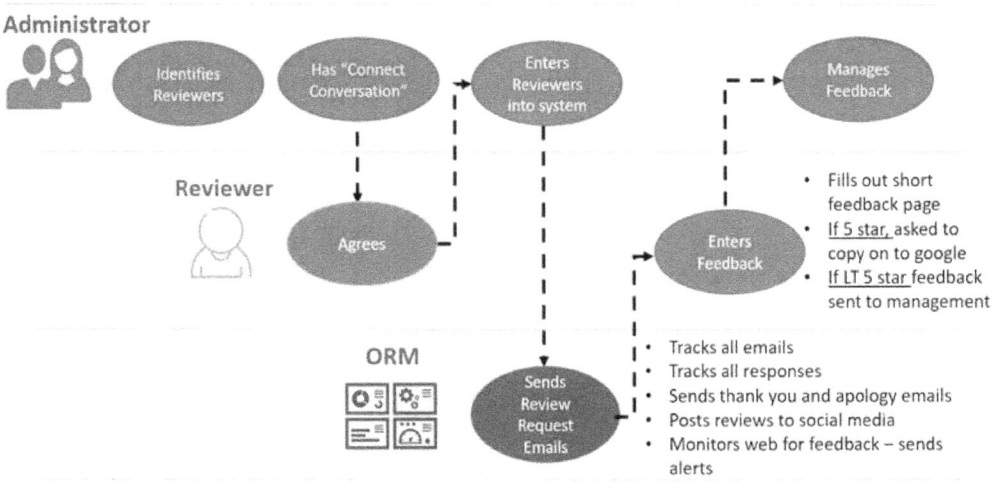

Basic Online Review Workflow

First, the employee or administrator of the system identifies customers to ask for reviews. Then, if they have direct access to the customer, they approach them with the simple Connect Conversation.

Once the customer agrees to give a review, the administrator enters the name, email address, and/or smartphone number into the ORMS. Some systems use email contacting software, some systems use text messaging and some use both.

The ORMS then takes over. It sends the customer an email or text review request.

It also tracks the customer's response and knows if they've responded. If not, it will make between 2-3 contacts with the customer spread over 2-10 days. These contacts are short, warm, professionally written emails or text messages reminding the customer about the review.

The emails or text messages contain a link that the customer clicks on. The link takes them to a form that collects their star rating, review comments, and then connects them to directories like Google, Facebook or Yelp, where they can leave the review online.

In cases where it's not feasible to contact the customer face-to-face, their contact information can be entered into the system, and the email is sent automatically requesting a review.

The ORMS doesn't stop there.

There are a variety of flexible functions in an ORMS. The full-functioned ones include options that will monitor the web for mentions and reviews, notify staff when new alerts have been left, and automatically post 4- or 5-star reviews directly to website and social media pages. An ORMS can also send out and collect customer survey information.

Posting reviews to website and social media pages is a very powerful marketing tactic. Website, blog or social media page visitors will see these reviews as they visit those pages. This can amount to a large number of free "testimonial ads" shown throughout the course of the year, limited only by the amount of page views.

A good ORMS will also special-handle negative reviews, alerting the owner or manager to take action when an unhappy customer comments, allowing an immediate and personal response by the company to address the problem.

Another benefit is that once set up, the ORMS functions operate with little or no staff effort. All that's necessary is for the staff to input the customer's information and respond to reviews. This is why an ORMS can be so effective in increasing the number of reviews and why it puts the business firmly in control of their own reputation destiny.

The Pet Resort That Became The Market Leader:
Using an ORMS, Bayside Pet Resort in Sarasota grew its reputation from just a handful of reviews a few years ago, to 185 Google reviews with an average 4.7 rating. Add to that 711 additional reviews that weren't posted to Google but were recorded as feedback/testimonials. Two additional company locations opening in the area have accumulated another 201 Google reviews under the same brand name. They've become the local market leader creating a reputation where large chain, and local competition is lagging way behind.

What's more, the ORMS posted the 4 and 5-star reviews – Google and feedback reviews - on their Facebook, Twitter, Google My Business, and Instagram accounts. The total number of times these reviews were seen by page visitors is now approaching 1M views.

The Senior Care Organization That Could
Capital Health Care operates 20 different nursing home, assisted living, independent living and home health care locations in Ohio and West Virginia. This industry is currently not as web-involved as the previous example (see the case study), so the number of reviews for businesses in this industry tend to be lower.

Despite that, Capital Health Care saw the potential in building an online reputation. So, we installed an

ORMS for them. They have now grown their online reviews from less than a dozen for all their locations a few years ago, to 154 Google reviews today. In just the last six months they've added an additional 150 feedback/testimonial reviews - not posted to Google, but posted by the ORMS to their web and social media pages. We estimate that between 25,000 and 50,000 web page and social media page visitors saw their 5-star reviews as they browsed - a nice reputation boost!

Capital Health Care is also an example of an organization that worked tirelessly to improve the quality of their services. As we pointed out earlier, that is job number one in reputation building. They've won numerous awards and 5-Star ratings from organizations like CMS (Centers for Medicare and Medicaid Services). They're solving the problem of getting more positive reviews in an industry that isn't quite as active in building online reputations and they're creating a strong brand image of trust – a priceless currency in their industry.

In summary, building a positive online reputation is a long-term strategy that will create an enduring brand and every business should have a well-thought-out method of reputation building that incorporates as many best practices as possible.

Always respond to positive and negative reviews professionally, and share reviews to social media and website pages.

Finally, consider using an Online Reputation Management System to multiply your efforts and shorten the timeline to a competitive advantage reputation.

It's Showtime!

"Your brand is what people say about you when you're not in the room."

Jeff Bezos

You've now started to take control of your reputation by making sure that the underlying  business is in tip-top shape and you're requesting and getting an increasing number of reviews. It's now time to market those reviews, using every channel available.

Marketing reviews is a strategy that lets the world know about your good reputation in a way that builds trust.

The Twin Levers of Online Reputation

Let's start the discussion on marketing your reputation with two influencers of online reputation: online content and social media.

How Valuable Online Content Grows Your Reputation

Organic searches are the millions of searches that are made every single minute in search engines by users who are looking for information or to solve a problem.

It could be in the form of a question such as, "How do I get rid of garden pests?" or just a few words for what they're searching for, such as "garden pest spray." When people enter queries like these into Google's search bar, Google will display Search Engine Results Pages (SERPs).

The lesson here is to create valuable content and post it everywhere you can on the web.

SERPs will display a combination of ads, organic content, local search results and other useful information, related to the search term and ranked in order of their value to the searcher, as defined by Google's RankBrain algorithm. For local businesses, they also display the average star rating and the number of reviews.

Having organic content that consistently ranks highly in Google's SERPs is a badge of authority. Blog posts, videos, articles or press releases are examples of content that a business would want to be found on the web. And how do they get found? By ranking highly for relevant search terms.

Google values time on site and bounce rates as important ranking metrics. And how does one improve in these metrics? Through interesting, entertaining, and useful content. The more they see people reading, watching, sharing, downloading, backlinking to and commenting on a particular piece of content, the more it defines it as high value content, and ranks it higher in search engine results for relevant search terms.

In this way, highly ranked content becomes an important part of online reputations. Highly ranked content will attract additional visits to the website, and social media pages where reviews are shown as well.

Not only does the content need to be valuable to users, but it needs to be delivered using sound Search Engine Optimization (SEO) principles such as relevant keywords, descriptions, header tags, etc. There's an article in the resources section that explains some of the more important SEO principles.

The lesson here is to create valuable content and post it everywhere you can on the web. It takes time and work to create content that builds the brand's reputation, but in many ways, sought-after content is the gold standard of online reputation. After all, this is why the internet was first created – as a way to share information of value to its users.

The latest information from SEO experts who test the Google algorithm says that it's more the quality of the content (and not the quantity) that's important.

How Social Media Helps (or Hurts)

Social media may influence online reputation even more than organic content, but in different ways.

There's long been a debate as to whether social media platforms like Facebook and Twitter influence search engine rankings, or if Google even indexes social media content in its search results.

Most of the experts such as HubSpot (see the article in the Resources section) seem to indicate an increasing willingness by Google to index Facebook and Twitter posts.

But one thing is certain: social media is an important part of an online reputation because it's how most brands engage and communicate with their customers and followers. Social media activity also increases website traffic – providing another way of elevating online reputations.

Think about it. Even if you have a website or published articles, would an online reputation feel complete without some social media presence? No, it wouldn't.

In my opinion every business should have at least a Facebook, LinkedIn, Twitter or Instagram account. Having a Facebook page lets people know that you're in the game. It says you believe it's important enough to give your customers, clients and patients an online place where they can see and learn who you are, communicate with you, and see what other people say about your brand or business.

One caveat: whatever platform you choose, just be sure to show some regular activity on it. There's nothing worse for a prospective customer than to visit a business page and see that the last post was two or six months ago or longer. A page like that only serves to disappoint visitors, and puts negative dents in online reputations.

> The primary benefit of GMB is that Google rewards its active listing owners with greater visibility and rankings in local search results

Although not considered to be a social media platform by everyone, Google My Business has emerged as the ultimate social media platform for local business. As indicated earlier, GMB allows businesses to post offers, news, videos, images, business information and, of course, the company's reviews. People can also ask questions and leave comments – just as you can on any other social media platform.

The primary benefit of GMB is that Google rewards its active listing owners with greater visibility and rankings in local search results. We've helped clients significantly increase their search engine rankings just by optimizing their GMB listing.

The Rise of Facebook Messenger

A few years ago, active users on Facebook Messenger exceeded users on Facebook pages. There are now more than 8 billion messages per month on this platform, and it's growing rapidly. It remains to be seen if this growth rate will continue, but Facebook has announced plans to make it the fastest, most used platform on the planet.

Importantly, chatbot technology has matured so that it works directly with Facebook Messenger to automate routine responses to page subscribers, and provide useful product and service information with much higher engagement rates than email. A chatbot creates an efficient Live Chat platform for people who want to talk to a human.

Consider adding a chatbot to manage your Facebook page messages. The automated, yet personable conversations in well-designed chatbots, will increase responsiveness to customers, strengthen engagement, and allow you to distribute loyalty-building content, with little staff effort and relatively low cost.

Done correctly, it's an engaging, conversational experience for the visitor, and gets them quickly down the path of becoming a customer.

Facebook Messenger marketing is a good supporting system for building an online reputation.

The twin levers of content creation and social media amplify a business's efforts to improve its products and services and create an online reputation that builds the brand.

Managing an online reputation through content production and social media is more than just creating a Facebook page or writing good webpage copy.

If you're wanting to use these levers to enhance a reputation, it will take time and work. Fortunately, it's not all-hands-on-deck-emergency type of work. It's more a steady drumbeat of content and social media engagement, performed with whatever resources are available.

Boosting Reviews For More Branding Power

Boosting reviews is a super strategy, particularly if you don't have a lot of reviews. Our company is an example. We purposely serve a smaller number of clients, and therefore we don't have a ton of Google reviews posted online. But the reviews we do have are great and are supported by non-Google testimonials from various social media platforms.

When we need it, we boost the visibility of Google reviews by running Facebook, Google and display ads, and uniquely in the headers of our social media pages - all showing selected 5-star reviews and branding info.

This is where retargeting display ads can exert the most power. We routinely run display ad campaigns for both our business and our clients that feature an excerpt from a 5-star review. The brand-building value of these review ads appearing in front of a targeted audience when they're surfing the web is priceless.

Creating a short video of 5-Star reviews makes great ad content for Facebook or YouTube ads. YouTube ads are some of the best ad bargains on the web right now.

A social media header strategy is an innovative one because it utilizes the as much as 50% of Facebook, Twitter, LinkedIn, Instagram and YouTube image header real estate. Think of these page spaces as online billboards. Unfortunately, the majority of businesses either leave them blank, or don't leverage them as a place to display visitors' testimonials and related marketing messages.

Changing these headers 5-10 times per year, with new messages each time, also means that most followers are notified of the new header change – and that means additional traffic to social media pages, and ultimately to the website. Your notified, now curious followers will want to go to your page to see what's different.

This is a much more powerful tactic than the current trend of Facebook video headers. Why? Because not all social media platforms support video headers, and although they're eye-catching, most owners won't change them out very often. Video headers don't lend themselves to frequently changes with consistent brand messages across all five social media platforms.

There's a link in the resources section that allows you to create a free social media header.

Local Marketing Power - Google My Business

Google My Business deserves a special discussion. *There isn't a more powerful marketing ally for local business than GMB.* Over the last few years it has become a marketing must. Part social media platform, part directory and part search engine, it adds new features every year.

Special GMB features that connect with local marketing efforts are:

▸GMB displays reviews and star ratings along with relevant business information (business name, address, phone number, web address, hours of operation and more)

▸GMB is closely connected to Google Maps

▶The ability to easily respond to reviews through the dashboard

▶The ability to post those reviews on the GMB platform and advertise them for greater visibility

▶A free website feature that integrates with GMB posts and helps in search engine rankings

▶Regular posts help elevate search engine rankings, bringing the reviews and star rating with it

Make sure to take these actions on your GMB listing:

▶Claim and verify your GMB listing - there are thousands (maybe even millions) of businesses that have not yet verified with Google

▶Make sure all business information is complete and accurate

▶Post regularly to GMB. Posting positive reviews online is one of the few sources of free advertising.

▶Set up the free GMB website even if you have a great site of your own

The next image is an example of a well-crafted GMB listing:

page viewers sees the page content and simultaneously sees the social proof of 5-star reviews written by their customers.

Employee Engagement

One of our clients uses reviews as recognition for the employees who asked for, and worked hard to achieve, good reviews from customers. Send a copy of outstanding reviews around in the company newsletter, or company communications, to acknowledge the employees and inspire others to do the same.

Brand Journalism – It's More Than Just Pretty Golden Stars

Brand journalism is an umbrella term for creating content that establishes a business as a trusted authority. There are many ways to do this. Here are some suggestions:

- ►Blogging
- ►Website content creation
- ►Sharing reviews and testimonials
- ►Regular video postings to a YouTube Channel
- ►Regular news releases articles
- ►Regular postings to social media
- ►Podcasting
- ►Speaking engagements

All of these are about creating content that customers want to consume. In so doing, it gives a business the opportunity to share a brand message and demonstrate why they're a good choice to do business with.

If there isn't good content about you and your company as part of your marketing strategy, it's up to you to start creating it. As noted earlier, content is one of the twin levers for building an online reputation.

But what if you're in a business that doesn't lend itself to brand journalism? I'll answer that with another question: What business reputation wouldn't benefit from creating regular, positive, useful information and broadcasting it to their ideal customer?

If you run a restaurant, recipes, menus, food images, live videos and testimonials become great brand journalism content. If you're a roofer, homeowner tips for roof care, new materials for roofing, state and federal special funding programs, and roofing innovations become your content.

What about dentists and doctors? Wouldn't customers and clients be interested in regular information on how to keep themselves healthy?

Wouldn't any business that became known for sharing this kind of information create a reputation of trust and stand out from their competitors?

You get the picture – whatever the business, its reputation would benefit from brand journalism –the online "fuel" for building the brand.

Let's talk in a little more detail about a few brand journalism strategies.

Blogging

A blog is a collection of content – articles, videos, audio – that the author posts regularly to, usually on their website, or website blog page. Blogging has been around for many years, and it's still an important way to build a reputation as an authority. A blog works to help your online reputation in two ways.

First, it helps establish you or your business as an expert in your field.

On your own blog you can talk not only about the products and services you offer, but also about anything in your industry. You can address concerns, give tips, offer advice, and do so much more to show that you are the expert in your industry. And when customers are looking for your product and/or service, you're top of mind.

Secondly, creating regular blog content improves search engine rankings for relevant keywords. With higher search engine rankings, people will find the business more often when using relevant search queries, and discover all those beautiful golden stars!

Podcasting is another form of brand journalism that reinforces the company's reputation. Podcasting is a way to broadcast content to an audience on the web in live or recorded audio form. It has become an affordable platform for just about any business.

Social Media Engagement

True social media engagement is harder to come by these days because of the high level of competition for customer attention. Engagement involves not only regular posting, but posting content that is valuable enough that people want to share, comment on and "like".

Nowhere is the struggle for a business to improve its reputation more evident than in social media. Why? Because of all the different platform options, and the time it takes to build engagement in any one platform.

If you want to be active in social media, you'll want to make sure you're on the biggest two – Facebook and Instagram. Of course, as a local business, you'll also need to be on GMB.

If your business lends itself to video media, YouTube and Instagram are two of the highest engaging social media platforms around. But you may want to create a presence on Twitter and LinkedIn as well.

Every company has to choose how best to put their social media resources into the best channels. For most small to mid-sized businesses (and even large ones) it's not an option to develop all of these channels. I know of no company that is doing them all well (nor do they need to).

Once you have your chosen social media channels set up, start engaging! By posting quality content regularly and interacting with people, you'll grow your following, increase the chances of improved search rankings and develop a greater online presence.

Some current social media trends that many are seeing success with are:

- ►Facebook Messenger Chatbots

- ►Live Video Streaming (especially YouTube, but
- ►Facebook and Instagram as well)

- ►Facebook Groups

- ►Google My Business

- ►Instagram and Instagram stories

- ►Using social media headers to deliver marketing messages

Website Content

Your website is a 24/7 salesperson. Ranking on the first page of Google is a dream of many businesses. But should it be?

Truthfully, most businesses don't care if they're on the first page of Google. They care about getting their phone to ring and acquiring more customers, patients or clients. However, their chances of doing that are much better if they're positioned highly for relevant searches.

SEO activity is usually foremost on the minds of companies wanting to improve their site's online presence. And there's good reason to work on that, because SEO drives traffic to the website. More traffic will boost page rankings and those hard-won golden stars can be shown to more people.

Website content on the other hand is what converts traffic into leads and buyers. An underutilized tool across most industries is a website content audit. These audits look for consistent and clear brand messaging, clarity and visibility of key messages, strength of calls to action, and other elements. We use a 35-point audit of website content factors.

When people engage with interesting or valuable content on your web pages, Google sees this as page engagement - one of their important ranking factors, maybe even more important than traffic numbers.

Copy is what makes pages interesting, "sticky" and valuable to the visitor.

Start The Presses!

What you're looking for is good press to spread your reputation far and wide. How about piggy-backing on hundreds of authority websites – all carrying backlinks to the website?

This can be done through syndicated press releases. Through a press release, you're able to "get the (brand) word out" to the public and get them talking about your product and your company.

This not only gives you a chance to show people how great you are, but also gets people to your blog, website, and social media channels. The more people talk (in a good way) and know about you, the better your online reputation will be.

One myth that needs to be exposed is that you need spectacular news to write a press release. Not true! We routinely write client press releases to cover such things as executive promotions, product changes, yearly results, employee hiring and much more. Every one of them is picked up by about 500 authority sites around the web. A series of 4-6 press releases gives your site a nice traffic and SEO boost.

For examples of press release topics, you'll see a link to our free report *"106 Reasons To Write A Press Release"* in the Resource Section.

White Papers and special reports are unique forms of brand journalism that establish authority and at the same time create a lead magnet where people trade their contact information for a copy of the white paper. White papers and special reports are especially useful when you have a product or service that is more complex, or technical, thus needing more education for prospects.

A Real Estate Brokerage Shows Its Stuff

RE/MAX Platinum Realty of Florida is a five-office real estate brokerage in the Sarasota Gulf Coast area. A few years ago, they had a problem – they didn't show up in the first 20+ pages of Google's search results for terms like "Sarasota real estate agents" "Venice real estate", or "Sarasota Real Estate".

Anyone involved in real estate marketing can tell you that real estate keywords are some of the most competitive and difficult to rank for on the web. But after a few years of consistent work on their online presence, you can now find them in the top three of Google' local 3-box for these same keywords.

How much additional business comes from appearing on Google's first search page? It's not possible to say with accuracy. But we do know that 75% of the clicks will go to the first page of search results. We think of being on Google's first page or in the 3-boxaslike having your business located prominently on the busiest street in town.

For a real estate broker, it only takes a few additional home listings at 6% commission or attracting a few more high-producing agents to make a noticeable profit difference, and strengthen its brand name throughout the area.

The process we used to make these gains wasn't magical. It consisted of:

► Adding an ORMS and collecting more online reviews

► Weekly posts to GMB and Google+ (yes, used correctly Google+ carried great ranking power even though Google has since shut that platform down)

► Adding backlinks and citations pointing to the website

► Making sure NAP (Name, Address, and Phone Number) across the web was accurate and consistent

► Optimizing website elements and content

► Optimizing the YouTube Channel with informative videos

► Creating a syndicated press release series

It was rare if the ongoing workload to do this exceeded more than a few hours per week. Faster results could be achieved with additional effort.

> Brand journalism is an umbrella term for creating content that establishes a business as a trusted authority.

Google sees these steady reputation and branding activities as adding value to its user's experience, and rewards the business with higher search engine rank.

In summary, spend some time growing the numbers of positive reviews, strengthening your Google My Business listing, and showing positive reviews and testimonials everywhere online.

Add a few solid brand journalism activities that fit your business model and available resources. When combined with high quality products and services, you'll soon become a Jedi in your business niche, sporting an average star rating approaching 5 stars.

Isn't that the kind of online reputation you really want?

More to the point, don't you think this work will bring you more followers, more subscribers, more buzz about your products and more business?

I'm betting it would.

Manage Your Reputation

"In a digitally connected world, a byte
of data can boost or bite your brand."

-Bernard Kelvin Clive

Now that you've begun to improve your star rating, and market your reputation on social media and your website, you're done, right? Well, no – you're never *done.*

Scour The Internet

Now you have to continuously track your online reputation to respond, to intervene when necessary – like responding to reviews. You don't want to let it go untracked for a number of years and then end up unknowingly with a bad or non-responsive reputation.

Luckily, you don't need to be online every day manually searching for your keywords and trying to find comments people have left about your company. There are many great tools you can use to track your online reputation and here are just a few:

►**Feedreader**. Feedreader is a platform that will let you keep track of websites and will automatically update you whenever something new is posted to those sites. This can be used to keep track of review sites and competitor sites that might be saying something about you. Just spend five minutes a day going through the feeds and looking for your company's name to see if there's anything negative that needs to be dealt with.

►**Technorati**. Technorati is similar to Feedreader. Just set up specific keywords or websites, and you'll be notified any time there's a mention of your website.

►**Google Alerts**. Google Alerts lets you set up certain keywords that you'd like alerts for. If you enter your company's name into Google Alerts, you'll get an alert every time it's mentioned online. You can also set up Google Alerts for any comments or videos that you find, or content that you've uploaded yourself. Any time there's any activity with that content, you'll be notified immediately.

►**Yahoo Alerts.** This is very similar to Google Alerts, but you should use this as well, as it will cover one more search engine for you.

►**Yahoo Answers.** This is an interesting feed. Yahoo Answers is designed specifically to accept users' questions, and have other users answer them. For business owners, this is useful because you can set it up so that Yahoo Answers will find any questions that are being asked about your company and will send you an alert when a question has been asked. You can then promptly reply to it and keep up your online reputation!

►**Twitter Search**. The # search function in Twitter is very useful. This allows you to search all of Twitter for mentions of your company and/or product and respond to them within seconds.

►**Social Mention.** To save yourself some time, you can use Social Mention which, as its name implies, will search across several different social networks and alert you every time there's a mention of your name, brand or product.

►**Boardreader.** There are message boards and forums out there where people are talking about your company and you might not even know about it. Boardreader will scour those forums and message boards, search for the keywords you've set up and have an alert sent to you. You can get your results from a certain date, a certain forum or based on relevancy.

As you search through different readers and alert systems, you'll find the ones that work best for you. The important thing is that you have the ability to search social networks, websites, keywords, comments and forums. Doing so will keep you in tune with what's being said about you online.

Make Your Browser Anonymous To Discover The Truth

Sometimes, you'll want to hide your location and identity during a manual search process. Doing so prevents search engines from using past search history to give you results they think you'll be most interested in.

Your search history includes your location, previously visited websites and topics or industries you're most interested in. While this works well for users who want to use the same or similar category of searches, it may not provide the most complete information for those who need to do a broad search for online reputation mentions.

In order to properly assess your reputation, you need to see things as others see you, not the way you see you. In order to do that, you'll need to log out of any search engine accounts and disable personalized search. After doing that, search engines won't know who you are and will start to deliver results just as they would to any other user.

Using browser options like Google Chrome's Incognito function can help by not allowing search history to influence search results. Alternatively browse in private sites like DuckDuckGo.com or Startpage.com

What To Look For

Once you're anonymous, you can then go looking for your company, product or service reputation. You're not going to find everything that everyone's saying about you with just one search, so be prepared to spend some time on this task.

There are several things you'll want to search for. Here are some ideas to get you started:

- ►Company name

- ►Brand name

- ►Product name(s)

- ►Names of key personnel or staff members

- ►Company name, important keywords, e.g. "Best tire cleaner, Wilmington Tire Company" and "Worst tire cleaner"

It's very important to make sure that your business Name, Address and Phone number (NAP) is accurate and consistent across the web. Google will often consider a listing for the same business on different directories with one using "Avenue" in its name, and the other using "Ave." as *different* businesses. For good search engine rankings, you don't want Google confused about who you are.

If you run across errors, contact the directory or login and fix it

Remember that in order to find everything there is to know about you online, you can't limit yourself to just one search engine. In addition to searching for the above terms, remember to use the other search engines and metasearch engines (search engines that compile results from other search engines). Some of these are:

- ►Google Images
- ►Google Video
- ►Google
- ►Bing
- ►Yahoo
- ►Ask
- ►Dogpile
- ►ZapMeta

You can also do a search for "search engines" and "metasearch engines" to find more places to assess your online reputation.

The online scorecard tool we use for our clients to find what is being said around the web is another example of a time-saving way to access directories and search engines for comments, mentions, reviews, feedback and NAP (Name, Address, and Phone Number) errors. The next image shows an example for a law firm assessment:

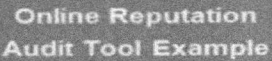

Online Reputation
Audit Tool Example

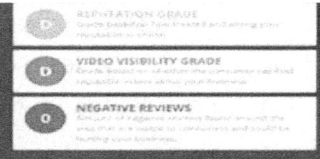

McKay Law Firm
1904 Manatee Ave W Suite 300, Brade...
Bradenton, FL 34205

Phone (941) 251-4951
Website allaw.mckay-law.com
Category

Loading...

FIX ALL LISTINGS

WHY AREN'T YOU #1 IN YOUR MARKET?

WHO IS GETTING ALL YOUR BUSINESS? Below are some key indicators that need to be addressed so you can get more visibility for your company and beat your competition.

Keyword: LAWYER, BRADENTON, FL

Mackey Law Group, P.A.
★ ★ ★ ★ ★ (9 Reviews)
Lawyer
1402 3rd Ave W (941) 746-6225

1st Place
Google Ranking

The Pendas Law Firm
★ ★ ★ ★ ★ (0 Reviews)
Lawyer
1201 6th Ave W #501d (941) 800-0000

2nd Place
Google Ranking

Map   Satellite

Below Are Some Reasons Why You Are Not Ranking #1 In Google

 CITATIONS   **LISTINGS**   **WEBSITE**

0   **4**   **6**   **0**   👎

Low Amount   Inaccurate   No Reviews   Google Reviews   Poor Optimization

LEARN MORE ABOUT THESE ISSUES

D- VISIBILITY GRADE

EXPLANATION   To get more customers your business needs to be listed on all the major directories and your information needs to be 100% accurate so that customers can call you and find your location.

DIRECTORY	BUSINESS NAME	ADDRESS	PHONE	REVIEWS	STATUS
Google	Mc Kay Law Firm	1904 Manatee Ave W Suite 300, Bradenton	(941) 251-4951	0	✓ CORRECT
Bing	Mckay Law	1904 Manatee Ave W Ste 300	(941) 251-4951	0	✓ CORRECT
Yahoo	Mckay Tabesa - Mckay Law Firm	1904 Manatee Ave W #300	(941) 800-7256	0	FIX LISTING ✗ Incorrect Name
Yelp					SCAN AGAIN
				0	FIX LISTING ✗ Not Found
				0	FIX LISTING ✗ Not Found
				0	FIX LISTING ✗ Not Found

VISIBILITY SCORE SUMMARY

ERRORS FOUND	16
LISTING ERRORS	89%

CORRECTIVE ACTION - You will need to make sure you register an account with each directory and claim your listing. Once you have claimed your listing you can go into each account and update your company information to your current information. Contact us today and we can give you a free guidance that will show you how to do it yourself, or we can help you do it ... **CONTACT US**

REPUTATION GRADE

EXPLANATION   Your business has 0 listings with reviews and 6 without any reviews. Not having any reviews or positive reputation associated with your listing will negatively impact your reputation grade. Studies show that without 6-10 reviews associated

78

The scorecard captures data from 33 major directories and social mentions. It shows how visible online the business is, its NAP errors, online reviews, and makes a comparison to the leading competitors.

While 33 directories may be a small percentage of the total universe of directories, it covers all the major and custom directories. You'll get an accurate look at your overall online reputation and your competitors'.

A link to use this free tool is in the Resource Section, or do a Google search for "online reputation assessment tools".

Know What's Being Said About You On Social Media

Social media plays a big role in any individual's or business's online reputation. This makes monitoring social media extremely important.

Once you start monitoring social media mentions, it's important to engage commenters in conversation. It's one of the best things about social networking – you get to communicate directly with your customers and potential customers in a way that everyone can see who you are.

You can also search on social media using a #(your company) search.

There are tons of social media websites and more are starting up every day. Checking each of them individually might seem near impossible. Luckily, there are tools available that reduce the manual search work involved.

These tools track what people mention about your business across the web. Most have some combination of free and paid services. Some will compare your business to competitors, or even compile statistics so you can compare negative and positive reviews at a glance.

You can do a quick search for monitoring platforms, but here are a few to check out to get you started:

- ►HootSuite
- ►Reviewpush
- ►Social Mention
- ►Keyhole
- ►Addict-o-Matic
- ►Brandwatch
- ►Buzzsumo
- ►Google Alerts
- ►HowSociable

Continuously tracking comments and mentions on the web allows you to rapidly respond, building a reputation as a business totally in tune with the people who use its products and services.

Formulating Your Reputation Brand Plan

So now you've searched compiled stats, reviews and mentions. Now what do you do with all of this information?

This is where you start assessing how to improve your reputation

While there's no objective rule for determining whether an online reputation is good or bad, a few simple, common-sense rules of thumb can determine what actions are necessary:

1) If your number of reviews is not at least 50% more, and your average star rating is not appreciably better than your local and national competitors, your online reputation needs work. Start a process to build the number of reviews and average star rating.

2) Do a Google search for your brand name. If there aren't at least 10-20 results and links to your site, and/or they don't present your business as an authority business, consider implementing brand journalism efforts.

3) If there are few social mentions or engagements on your social media business pages, pick a social media platform or two and spend a little time each week building engagement.

But what should you do to improve it in a way that tops competition?

Let the Reputation Brand Model shown in the next image be a simple guide to creating basic strategies and actions for improvement.

Reputation Brand Model

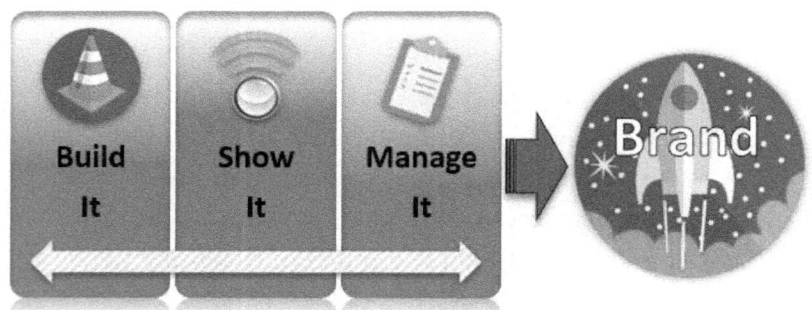

This model summarizes the entire approach contained in *Own Your Reputation!*

"***Build It***" includes putting in place best practices for collecting and responding to reviews.

*"**Show It**"* represents the steps to market your 5-star reviews through web, social media, and brand journalism.

*"**Manage It**"* includes the auditing and monitoring of the web for reviews and mentions, and protecting your reputation against problems. It also includes the continuous collection of reviews.

It's a continuous process that if done well and with purpose will provide rocket fuel for your brand's reputation.

With your team, generate goals for each of these broad areas, and develop a plan with specific tasks. Assign resources to achieve those goals.

Keep in mind that it's not necessary (or possible) to do everything at once. Steady work, applied with a determined plan and a goal of building an outstanding online reputation wins this race.

Handling Negative Reviews

No business is perfect, and there will be negative reviews on this journey. Accept that there's just no way to please everyone all of the time.

Negative reviews may be upsetting to read. But if handled correctly they can help you gain respect from prospective customers and differentiate your business from competitors. Always see them as an opportunity to improve your business. They can also identify specific improvements to better serve future customers.

And for goodness' sake, respond to each and every one of them (hopefully, it will only be a few). We've already seen what a powerful branding technique that is.

Responding to Negative Reviews

Remember to respond to each and every negative review online. Google loves to see businesses respond online to reviews. They see this exchange of conversation between customer and business as valuable engagement, and rewards these activities with higher search rankings.

Responding to reviews, particularly negative ones, is an art form. Here are 5 suggestions to adopt the perfect attitude before responding to a negative review:

5 Things You Should Know Before Responding to Negative Reviews:

1) Be Empathetic and Don't Get Defensive -

No matter how wrong the customer might be, or how badly you feel the urge to clarify how the customer is the one at fault – don't do it. Avoid a public online battle at all cost. A chippy online back and forth with a customer will cost you countless leads who may see your response as defensive and condescending. So, when you respond, always present yourself as empathetic and professional, and intensely interested in solving the complainer's problem.

2) Engage the Customer, Patient or Client – If you are not entirely sure what the complaint is about then engage the customer for more feedback about why they were dissatisfied. Ask them to call or visit with your business so you can get specifics on how you can make their experience more enjoyable and how you can make amends with the customer.

3) Create a Personal Dialogue – When you respond to customer reviews you want to sound like a real person. Too many companies make the mistake of responding to extremely personal reviews with a 1994 sterile press release type response. Be professional BUT be personal. Most people understand that any business can make mistakes, and they're far more ready to give it the benefit of the doubt if your responses are polite, and authentic. Responding professionally is the secret to turning a negative review into a brand-building interaction for all to see.

4) Know When to Say When - There are just some customers and some situations that you aren't going to be able to resolve to the satisfaction of the customer (for example, a customer who demands that you fire a specific employee). Be honest in your response and let them know that there are just some requests you can't honor. While a dissatisfied customer may not like this, potential customers reading your response will respect the honesty.

5) Refund, Discount or Free Offer – When dealing with a dissatisfied customer, the goal should be to get them back into the business so that the customer can see the error of their ways and change their negative review - or at least post a new, positive one. To get them back into the store offer a refund, discount or free offer when you respond to them. The small amount of money you spend on a special offer for a dissatisfied customer may save you thousands.

Protecting Your Online Reputation

While you might have built up your online reputation to something that you can be proud of, the work isn't over yet. You need to protect your hard-won online reputation. Sometimes, you'll need to protect your reputation against more serious threats. Here are a few situations you may find yourself in:

Get Rid of Unfair and False Negative Reputation Factors

Part of building a more positive reputation is getting rid of any false, misleading or unfair reviews. Doing so will give your online reputation a real boost.

If there's false information floating around in cyberspace about your company, it needs to be taken down immediately. In order to try and get it taken down, you'll typically need to report it directly to Google or the directory in which the false information is appearing.

You'll need to ask them to remove the negative review, and provide a strong argument and any evidence possible that proves the negative review is not true. For instance, if the statement is an opinion such as "their bathroom was disgustingly dirty ", it's not likely that the review will be taken down.

But if the statement is something that's based on fact, such as "they failed their last health inspection" and you can provide certificates and documents that prove the statement to be untrue, it is likely that the complaint will be taken down.

You'll likely be able to reply to the person who made the complaint, but sometimes it will be strictly between you and the website owner.

When dealing with a trusted association or organization within your industry, ask to have an unfair negative review taken down. Let them know that you've permanently corrected the problem or prove that it never really existed in the first place.

If the organization is related to your business, there may be additional benefits to join the organization.

Report and take down hate sites
Online trolls, emboldened by their anonymity, can still put up hate sites to attack your company, products or services.

In recent months, it's been getting more difficult for them to carry this out, as the major platforms get serious about banning these kinds of activities.

Most web host and social media platforms have policies in place to take down hate sites. There's usually a complaint or abuse form that can be filled out and submitted. Blogging platforms don't like taking down their users' sites, so provide plenty of proof of untruthful statements or wrongdoings.

Legal action is always available if the hosting platform doesn't help. That path, however, can be expensive. Sometimes a simple letter from an attorney might be enough to get the host to take you a little more seriously.

Instead of legal action, it may be best to reply professionally online to these reviews and then make the effort to go get your next 10 or 100 positive reviews.

Reclaim a squatted domain name

A squatted domain is a domain, bought by a person not associated with your company, that contains your branded name or something very close. People buy these domains in order to make large profits by selling them back to you. They may or may not use them to spread false or damaging information about your business.

Unless the domain name is under trademark, there aren't many options to reclaim a squatted domain name except to pay whatever the owner is asking.

If you can show that there's been trademark infringement, you can get the website taken down and then purchase it from a domain registrar when it becomes available. If this is your route, get familiar with the steps outlined in the Uniform Domain-Name Dispute-Resolution Policy (UDRP).

Use privacy settings

Social media is an effective brand-building tool, but it can share much more information than you ever intended. Now, thanks to public pressure, Facebook and other social media platforms are tightening security and privacy policies, which is a good thing.

Make sure you understand and adjust your privacy settings to the level that you're comfortable with. For example, you could make your page "invitation only" or set it up so that comments are moderated and approved before they are posted.

These privacy settings are important because they can alert you every time someone says something about your company, and prevent you having negative comments sitting online for days or weeks without your knowledge.

You'll also need to do the same with website security and privacy settings, as will your web host, to protect it from hackers, who can easily destroy a company's online reputation.

In recent years, GDPR (General Data Protection Regulation) has become important. This regulation requires a business to notify visitors that cookies are being used and give them an option to control what personal information is being tracked. Although it's not a law in the US, if you do business with people in Europe, it's a requirement. Most experts feel it will be a requirement in the US in the future.

Create A Feedback Site To Deal With Complaints
This doesn't mean trashing your own company all over Twitter, or having staff post negative reviews on review sites. A feedback site is simply having a specific place online where customers can go if they have a complaint or an issue with your company.

When people are presented with this option, they usually appreciate the gesture to collect feedback from them – they feel as though they're actually being listened to.

The advantage to the business is that they'll have one place online where they can collect customer feedback and manage negative reviews. However, it doesn't prevent people from leaving a review on Google without interacting with your feedback site.

If this is a solution you'd like to try, create a website, totally dedicated to customer complaints. Title it something cute such as "[nameofcompany]sucks.com" and then create a playful landing page that says something like, "Hi! Tell us why we suck!" This then becomes an open forum for people to leave complaints or ideas on how you could improve your product or service.

Make sure that comments are moderated before being posted, and that everyone is being respectful of one another. Never allow swearing, threatening, hateful, rude or offensive behavior.

Listen to constructive criticism
Setting up a complaint site of your own, and making sure you are active across all social networks, won't do you any good if you're not listening to what people are saying.

As a business owner, you're proud of the business you've built and the products or services you're offering to your customers. It's natural to feel defensive, frustrated and somewhat angry when a customer says something unflattering about them. But resist the temptation to "strike back" when something negative is said.

Instead, listen with an open mind, try to address the customer's concerns in a friendly manner and offer them something in return for their trouble. If you remain level-headed with the customer, you'll win them over no matter how angry they are. And they might even become one of your most loyal customers because they appreciate how you handled the situation!

Conclusion

A good reputation is more valuable than money."

- Publilius Syrus

Smartphones and countless internet sites have given every consumer the ability to both leave reviews and read what other reviewers say. This has made online reviews more a part of buying decisions than ever and they'll continue to increase in importance.

An online reputation will be either a trust builder or a trust detractor. Either way it will be part of the brand's

Improving an online reputation is really about building trust with current and potential clients, patients and customers. People want to spend their hard-earned money with businesses that they can trust to provide the best in products and services. Trust has become a valuable marketing currency worth its weight in gold to any brand.

An online reputation will be either a trust builder or a trust detractor. Either way it will be part of the brand's story.

The successful business of the future will understand the review game they're in, take control of it, and steadily improve it. Businesses are operating today in a web environment where every review (positive or negative) and its response gets spread at warp speed – a dynamic that isn't as forgiving as it was just 5-10 years ago.

Always think about it in the following way: Right at this very moment, people are talking about my company. What will they tell other people? What will they write in their reviews? The answers to these fundamental questions matter.

People believe Google reviews, and they're much more likely to try and stay with a 4.8-star business than a 3.5-star business. Wouldn't you agree?

Elements like search engine rankings, brand strength, social media presence and authority content also play a part in creating your reputation.

In this book, we've attempted to lay out a case that growing, marketing and managing your reputation is the framework of success, with the number of reviews and the average star ratings being the focal point.

As the case study shows, even the most difficult of review situations can be improved. And it can be improved with steady effort using some of the best practices outlined in previous chapters. In my view, it comes down to these factors:

- ▶ The choice to take control of your own reputation

- ▶ The choice to make online reputation a business priority

- ▶ The will to make it happen

- ▶ The system to grow, market and manage it

- ▶ The leadership to get it done.

Beginning the journey to improve an online reputation brings with it a huge additional benefit - the ability to learn how to improve the business by listening to feedback. Better products and services keep a business ahead of competitors.

Is it a tall task to improve? Maybe. ***But all it really takes is a commitment and consistent effort in bite-size pieces.*** In months from now, you could see improved results. In a year, three years or five years, you could look back and be proud of what you've built. By then, if you've been diligent, you'll undoubtedly be known for an enduring brand that people trust – and one that attracts business.

Automating the review process as much as possible will make it more efficient, but never forget that it's all about providing the best quality products and services for your clients, patients and customers.

The old saying that nothing changes without action is usually true, but not necessarily in the case of online reviews. An online reputation can quickly get worse without the business owner's action or knowledge. It might also get better, but no business can afford to leave that up to chance.

I'll end by repeating the reputation mantra because it reflects the spirit of this process and will guide your efforts:

Love your customers,

Respect your competitors,

Leverage your reputation with both.

I hope you've gotten some value from this book. I wish you success on your journey.

Senior Care Services Online Review Case Study

Background

Each year, online reviews as an organization report card are becoming more important in proving a company's reputation of trust. Why? Because over 90% of people now use online reviews to help make purchase decisions – this includes people searching for senior care services.

Overall, the entire senior care services sector has a challenge to improve in acquiring a larger number of 5-Star reviews. This sector has some of the most difficult challenges to collect reviews because of the relatively low involvement of seniors on the internet.

This report answers 3 questions:

1) What can be learned from other organizations in the senior care sector who are successfully getting online reviews?

2) What can senior care organizations do to increase their number of online reviews?

3) What can senior care organizations do to increase their number of feedback reviews?

To answer these questions, the **B2B Resource Team** sampled over 90 assisted living, nursing home and home health care organizations in Columbus, Dayton Chicago,

Cincinnati, Sarasota and San Diego for their number of Google reviews, average star rating. We read through over 650 of their reviews to determine as much as possible, their sources (friends and family, patients and employees).

Reading through hundreds of online reviews was even more instructive than we imagined in understanding the challenge of providing consistently high-quality senior care for patients and employees, and at the same time getting good online reviews.

We called the most successful of these locations and asked for them to share their approach to getting reviews. Some readily complied, others were strangely tight-lipped.

We also consulted with other experts in the online reputation field to get additional perspective on how to increase the number of online reviews in this sector.

All of this, plus a scan of the top 100 local senior care organizations for each keyword to determine the % of them with no reviews, have led to the perspectives in this report.

Part I – Evaluating Senior Care Services Organization Reviews

Note that the data collected is not large enough to be statistically significant. However, it does lead to important insights and perspective.

Top takeaways:

1) There are two categories of senior care organizations relative to online reviews – the adaptors figuring out how to solve the problem of online reviews for the benefit of their businesses, and the victims who are at the mercy of random negative reviews. Senior care organizations with dozens of reviews, approaching 5 stars, are building a competitive advantage. Overall the senior care services sector has a major challenge in creating a culture of consistent 5-Star reviews. This is evidenced by the frequent situation of both 1- and 5-Star ratings coming from the same facility.

2) Some Senior Care organizations get "Wow!" Grades. Organizations that respond to each and every review, positive or negative stand out with a Wow! factor. Responding to both positive and negative reviews in a warm, professional manner shows the world their care for customers, demonstrates customer service, and brands the voice of the company. It's in marked contrast to the vast majority who ignore their online reviews, and perhaps don't even know what people are saying about them. Both positive and negative reviews are treasure chests of learnings and ideas for service improvements.

3) TARGET 10.4.8. To become demonstrably better than local Dayton and Columbus competitors, a senior care organization needs to target for at least 10 reviews per location and an average Google Star Rating of 4.8 in 2018, and then build on that in future years. This has proven to be achievable based on the work done by some of the benchmark companies in this sample. A high volume of 5-Star reviews is important. As an example, an organization with just one 5-Star review is one bad review away from a 3- Star online reputation.

4) Emotions motivate people to write online reviews. Angry people write reviews without prompting. People that like the way they've been treated are generally happy to help and will go through a few inconveniences to do so – like signing up for a Gmail account. Curiously, many happy people have to be persuaded and reminded to write reviews.

5) A laptop for Mom. 7% to 9% of the reviews in this sample were left by people who were clearly patients. Likely there were more patients in this sample that could not be identified as such. The barrier to getting online reviews from elderly clientele because of low computer skills and experience is real, but shrinking. Senior care service organizations should not assume that the elderly can't leave reviews. Ask them for reviews. (2017 Pew research shows that 42% of adults over 80 use the internet, jumping to 60% in ages 75-79).

6) It's a family and friends affair. The senior care organizations that are best at collecting large numbers of high reviews tend to put a priority on collecting reviews from the patient's family and friends, friends of the company, and employees.

7) To the victor belong the spoils. There's a huge opportunity for senior care service organizations who learn how to deliver quality services and capture these experiences in the form of 5-Star online reviews. There are wide variations within this sector's review results. The senior care service organization that figures out how to do this well will have a real competitive advantage over local and regional competition for years to come.

Part II – Online Reputation Performance of Senior Care Organizations

To get an idea of the review results other companies are achieving, we looked at the first 10 senior care companies that appeared in local search results for nine different terms like "Columbus Ohio Home Health Care", "Dayton Ohio Nursing Homes", etc. and calculated the average number of reviews, and the average star ratings for that group. We also looked at the % of organizations with no reviews.

Home Health Care organizations - No. of reviews, star ratings, and review sources

The average for specific keyword groups is shown on the chart below. We picked a few locations outside of the Ohio geographical areas to add perspective.

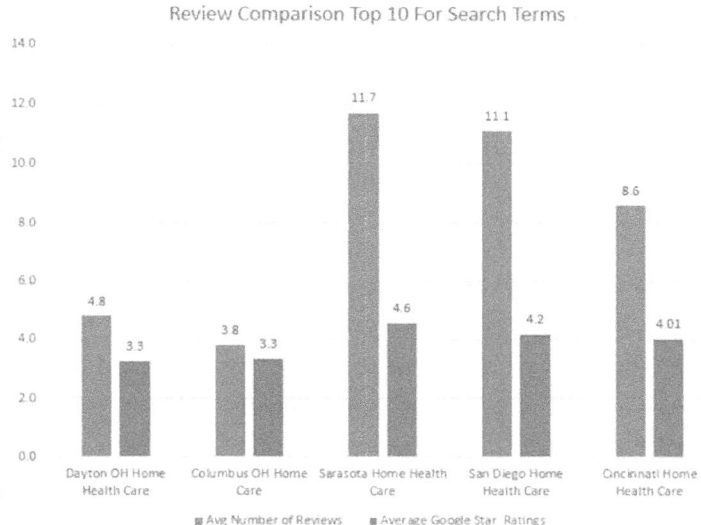

Review Comparison Top 10 For Search Terms

Benchmarking Home Care

There's lots of variability in the number of reviews and star ratings. A major factor seems to be how each organization approaches getting reviews. It's possible, even in this difficult sector to gather reviews and increase star ratings.

46% of the sampled companies had no reviews. This is quite high, and these companies will be easy to beat in the ratings/trust competition.

The reviews from Sarasota, San Diego, and Cincinnati are useful benchmarks of what's possible in-Home Health Care reviews.

It's clear from the current reporting that Home Health Care organizations have lots of upside improvement room in numbers of feedback and Google reviews per location, and in their ratings numbers. Implementing an online ratings system can provide a competitive advantage in getting both feedback reviews and Google reviews.

Who submitted these Home Health Care reviews?
Reading through reviews allowed us to record who the people were that were leaving reviews. We wanted to know if the majority were patients, family and/or friends, or employees. Although there is a high % of reviews with undefined sources in the chart below, it is my belief that a fair number of these were from family and friends, since overall, Family and Friends represent the largest identifiable group.

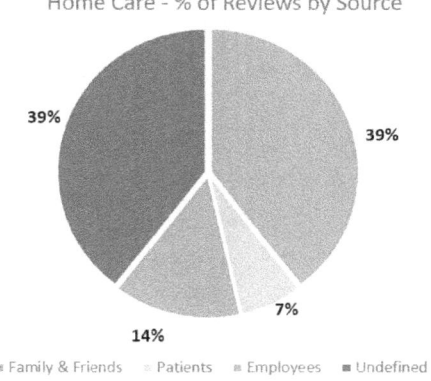

Home Care - % of Reviews by Source

39%   39%

7%

14%

■ Family & Friends   ▪ Patients   ■ Employees   ■ Undefined

Senior care services organizations - No. of reviews, star ratings, and review sources

This sample set, shown in the next graph includes nursing homes and assisted living facilities. The average number of reviews and overall ratings for this sample are higher than for Home Health Care. The average star ratings are about the same.

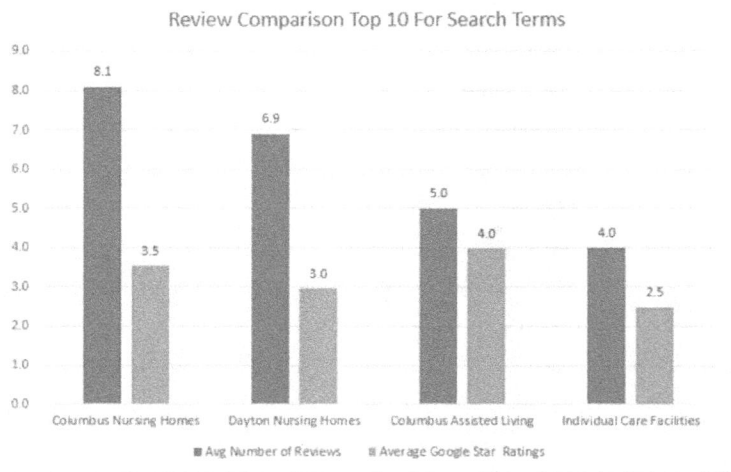

Review Comparison Top 10 For Search Terms

Who submitted these Senior Care services reviews?

Similar to the Home Health Care sample, the large undefined area in the next graph likely contains a high proportion of family and friends.

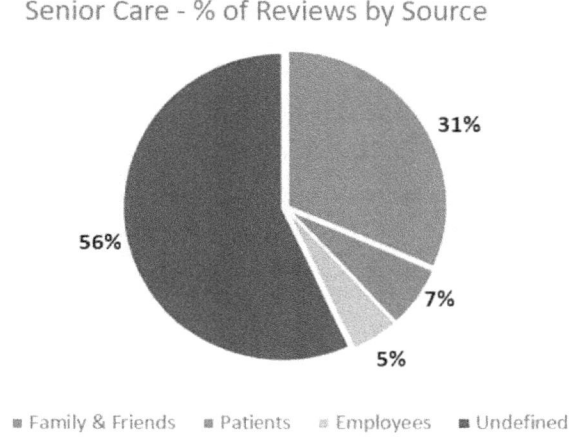

Senior Care - % of Reviews by Source

31%

56%

7%

5%

■ Family & Friends   ■ Patients   ▧ Employees   ■ Undefined

Best practices from the best performers in the sample groupings

We contacted the best performing organizations in this sample and asked them about their approaches to getting a large volume of 5-Star reviews.

In addition, we contacted others in the field of reputation management for additional ideas on the subject of improving review results.

This section summarizes these conversations, mostly centered on Home Health Care services, but learnings are applicable to senior care as well.

1) The organization commitment to the importance of reviews – positive and negative is clear. People at the highest levels of the organization are involved in getting reviews. In two cases the owners were the drivers of procuring reviews. They understand that reviews are good for online trust and improving their services.

2) There is a focus on getting reviews from family and friends vs. patients. Family and friends include people connected directly to the patients, and friends of the company itself.

3) Conscious effort is put into responding online to positive and negative feedback.

4) Home Health Care Provider Grannie Nannies of Sarasota (48 reviews, 4.9 stars) - says they proactively look for family and patients who have had positive experiences, and who have a Gmail account (they ask people directly if they have a Gmail account). (It isn't possible for them to post on to Google on behalf of any reviewer. They were aware of "black hat" purchases of reviews by some in the industry has that resulted in Google crackdowns – this could be a reason for some of the high "no review" numbers). The owner then follows up with them and asks them to leave a review. The owner coaches his employees to be involved in encouraging reviews by letting them know that this process means more business, and their pay is affected by it.

5) All Heart Home Care in San Diego (36 reviews, 4.9 stars) suggested that their secret may be in improving the quality of their services, and that happy families are willing to leave a review. They focus on asking the patient's family to submit reviews. They also have "Review Us' buttons on the website.

6) Home Helpers Home Care in Cincinnati (16 reviews, 5.0 stars) uses a third party (Best of Home Care) to survey their clients first. They use this as a tool for learning what needs improvement. For customers that have a positive experience, Home Helpers contacts them and asks them to leave a review. Their response rate for people leaving a review is less than 3%.

7) Using the simple, effective Connect Conversation to gets a better response from feedback requests. The reputation consulting secret: personal engagement with the potential reviewer prior to asking specifically for Google Reviews. The more family, friends and patients are asked using this simple engaging conversation, the more responses will occur.

Here's how:

a) Ask how their experience was

b) Ask if they wouldn't mind leaving a review on Google (if they're happy with service, they usually won't mind)

c) Give them a lofty reason why you're asking (if they need more motivation)

d) Before they leave, ask them if you can send them an email request with a link while they're here (sending this while they're in your presence is a subtle reinforcement for their commitment to respond)

e) Thank them and let them know that the team is looking forward to reading their review (giving them another reason why they won't want to let you down).

Some modification of this would look like:

How did it go today?

Great! Later today or tonight or whenever you get a chance, would you mind taking a few minutes to write a review for us on Google?

(Optional) The reason I ask is because when you do, it helps others learn about our business through your experience with us.

Before you go, may I send you an email with a link that makes it easy for you to write your review?

Thank you so much, and I want you to know that we're all really looking forward to reading your comments.

About The Author

Greg Jordan Greg received a BSME from Howard University in Washington, DC, and attended advanced business management classes at Xavier University in Cincinnati, Ohio. He is Google certified in Ads and Analytics.

Greg began his corporate career as an engineer and progressed to senior manager roles. He has been in corporate leadership positions for over 20 years, including Director of Engineering at Procter & Gamble, and Chief Innovation Officer with the Maytag Corporation.

He gained broad industry experience in leading organization change and new product launches in the Utilities, Pulp and Paper, Orange Juice Processing, Disposable Diapers, Health Care and Appliances industries.

He started the B2B Resource Team LLC, (formerly Peak Performance Solutions) in the year 2000 as a management consulting, marketing and advertising agency.

Greg's list of clients reflects a broad range of experience and capabilities. He has served large and small clients and nonprofits in the consumer products, sports, pet services, real estate, health care, senior care, engineering, and government sectors.

The B2B Resource Team's primary services are in reputation management, digital ad campaign management, business copywriting, consulting and marketing strategies, and social media projects. They partner with several marketing and service organizations.

His mission is to bring effective tools, methods and consulting to local businesses to improve their top-line and bottom-line performance.

Resources

Here are some resources to help in your online reputation work:

Free Online Reputation Scorecard

http://onlinescorecard.repgrader.com/reputationscore

Website Content Articles:

https://www.whatgrowsbusiness.com/

SEO Tips

https://blog.hootsuite.com/social-media-seo-experiment/

Press Releases:

https://www.whatgrowsbusiness.com/wp-content/uploads/2018/10/106Reasons.pdf

Reputation Repair

Google "malicious online review repair"

Free Social Media Header design

htpps://bit.ly/freesocialmediacover

Online SEO & Social Media Training Courses

https://www.udemy.com

Online Presence Solutions:

http://www.b2bresourceteam.com